Musical Instruments

written by Lucinda Cotter

Engage Literacy is published in 2013 by Raintree.
Raintree is an imprint of Capstone Global Library Limited, a company
incorporated in Engand and Wales having its registered office at 7 Pilgrim
Street, London, EC4V 6LB – Registered company number: 6695582
www.raintreepublishers.co.uk

Originally published in Australia by Hinkler Education, a division
of Hinkler Books Pty Ltd.
Text and illustration copyright © Hinkler Books Pty Ltd 2012

Written by Lucinda Cotter
Lead authors Jay Dale and Anne Giulieri
Illustrations on pp 4–24 (including world maps) by Gaston Vanzet
Edited by Gwenda Smyth
UK edition edited by Dan Nunn, Catherine Veitch and Sian Smith
Designed by Susannah Low, Butterflyrocket Design

Musical Instruments
ISBN: 978 1 406 26511 8
10 9 8 7 6 5 4 3 2 1

Printed and bound in China by Leo Paper Products Ltd

Acknowledgements

Cover images (left to right): © Ermess | Dreamstime.com; iStockphoto.com/ © jstudio; iStockphoto.
com/ © Jake Holmes; p5 bottom left: iStockphoto.com/ © Thomas Perkins; p5 bottom right (and Contents
page): iStockphoto.com/ © Craig Veltri; p6: © Mazor | Dreamstime.com; p7 (and back cover): © Ljupco
Smokovski | Dreamstime.com; p8: Stock Connection/SuperStock; p9: iStockphoto.com/ © jstudio;
p10: iStockphoto.com/ © Dale Hogan; p11 top right (and the title page): © Ermess | Dreamstime.com;
p11 bottom left: © Csproductions | Dreamstime.com; p12 top: © Dmitry Skutin | Dreamstime.com;
p12 bottom: Getty Images/Stockbyte; p13 top: iStockphoto.com/ © Shawn Gearhart; p13 bottom:
© Rui Matos | Dreamstime.com; p14 top: iStockphoto.com/ © Alexander Briel Perez; p14 middle:
iStockphoto.com/ © Jake Holmes; p14 bottom: iStockphoto.com/ © Rhoberazzi; p15 middle: © Nexus7 |
Dreamstime.com; p15 bottom: Lonely Planet Images/ Tim Barker; p16 top: © Kirill Vorobyev | Dreamstime.
com; p16 bottom: © Irabel8 | Dreamstime.com; p17 top: iStockphoto.com/ © MichaelSvoboda; p17
bottom: © Branislav Senic | Dreamstime.com; p18 left: © Bright | Dreamstime.com; p18 right: iStockphoto.
com/ © Jaimie Duplass; p19 top: Copyright Thomas R. Fletcher / www.proseandphotos.com;
p19 middle: istockphoto.com/ © Michael Flippo; p19 bottom: © Lucas Pablo Ponce | Dreamstime.com;
p20 left: iStockphoto.com/ © Linda Bucklin; p20 right: iStockphoto.com/ © Ayzek; p21 top: © Socrates |
Dreamstime.com; p21 bottom: © Emadrazo | Dreamstime.com; p22 left: iStockphoto.com/ © Gremlin;
p22 top right: © Neonnyc | Dreamstime.com; p22 bottom right (and Contents page): © Uatp1 |
Dreamstime.com; p23 top: DK Images; p23 bottom: Corbis/SuperStock.

Contents

Musical Instruments

People have been making music
with musical instruments
for thousands of years.
Almost any object that makes a sound
can be used to make music.

A *plastic* pipe didgeridoo

Didgeridoos made
from hollow trees

A hollow log drum

A drum made from wood and skin

A kazoo

A tambourine

There are musical instruments of all shapes and sizes in every country of the world.

5

Wind Instruments

Wind instruments are made of *hollow tubes*. They make a sound when you blow into them.

Israel

Shofar

The shofar is made from the *horn* of a *ram*.

It is used to call people together.

The shofar comes from Israel.

Trumpet

The first trumpets were made in Egypt
a long time ago. They were made
of animal horns, *bones* or *bamboo*.
Today, the trumpet is made of *brass*.
It has buttons (valves) that are pressed
to make the sound go up
or go down.

Egypt

Didgeridoo

The didgeridoo comes from Australia.
It is made from a hollow tree or branch.
The didgeridoo can make many different
kinds of sounds.

Australia

Recorder

A recorder is made of wood or *plastic*.
It has seven finger holes and one *thumb* hole.
You make music by blowing
into the *mouthpiece* and placing your fingers
on different holes.
The first recorders
were made hundreds
of years ago
in Europe.

Europe

Drums

People all over the world make music with different kinds of drums. Thousands of years ago, people made drums by *stretching* animal skins over hollow logs.

They found that by hitting the skins with their hands or sticks, they could make different sounds and different *beats*. The harder a drum is hit, the louder it sounds.

Many countries

Djembe

The djembe is an African drum made of wood and animal skin. It is usually played with the hands.

Western Africa

Kettledrum

The kettledrum is one
of the instruments in an *orchestra*.
It is like a big *bowl*
with animal skin stretched
over the top.
It is played with special sticks
called mallets.

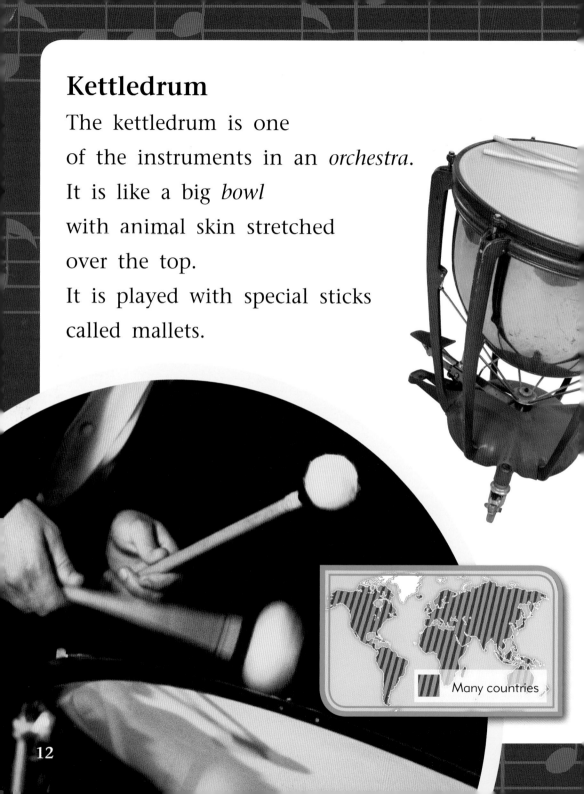

Many countries

Cymbals

Tom-toms

Snare drum

Bass drum

USA

Drum Kit

Drum kits were invented
in the United States of America in 1935.
With a drum kit, one person can play
many different drums at the same time.

String Instruments

Most string instruments are made of wood. The strings are stretched along a hollow body. You make music by *plucking* the strings or sliding a *bow* across them.

Violin

Violins were first made in Italy. They are an important part of an orchestra.

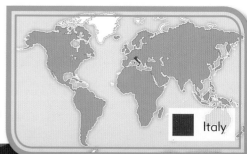

Italy

Violins have four strings, which are made of *steel* or *nylon*. The bow moves across the strings to make music.

Neck

Strings

Bow

Oud

The oud came from Arabia a long time ago. The body of the oud looks like a *watermelon* cut in half. It has eleven strings and a short neck.

Arabia

Guitar

The guitar has a long neck and strings that can be *strummed* or *plucked*. The one you see here is called a classical guitar. It has six nylon strings. The first guitars were made in Europe about 500 years ago.

Europe

Electric Guitar

The electric guitar is made of wood and *metal,* and has a long neck. It uses electric power to make the sound louder. The electric guitar is often used in a *rock band.*

Xylophone

The xylophone is made of wooden bars of different sizes.

A different sound is made as you hit each bar with a mallet.

The first xylophones were most likely made in Africa.

Africa

Central America

Marimba

A marimba is like a xylophone, but it usually has more wooden bars. It comes from Central America.

Keyboard Instruments

Keyboard instruments have a row of *keys* that are played with both hands. Each key makes a different sound — from a low to a high sound.

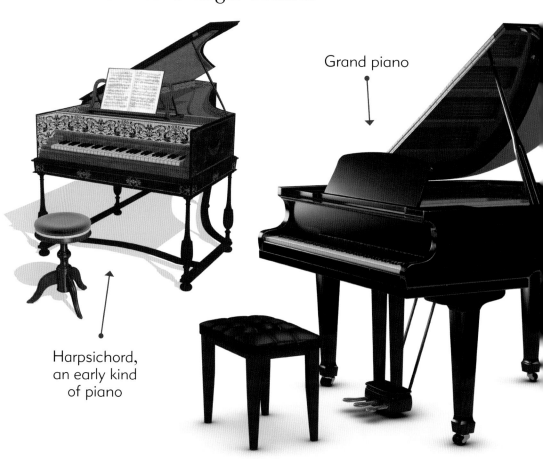

Grand piano

Harpsichord, an early kind of piano

Piano

Pianos have 88 keys — some are black and some are white. There are lots of strings inside a piano. When you press the keys, little hammers hit the strings and make musical sounds.

The first piano was made in Italy about 300 years ago.

Playing a piano

The inside of a piano

Italy

Electric Keyboard

An electric keyboard has keys just like a piano, but it does not have strings or hammers. It has a computer inside to make music. The electric keyboard is often used in a rock band.

Junk Music

Sometimes people make
musical instruments
from old things.

You can make music from things
that you blow, or bang or pluck.
This is called junk music.

You could make your own junk music.
You could use lids, spoons, pots and pans,
or plastic bottles filled with rice.

People have always
loved to play
and hear music.

Music is
an important
part of life.

Picture Glossary

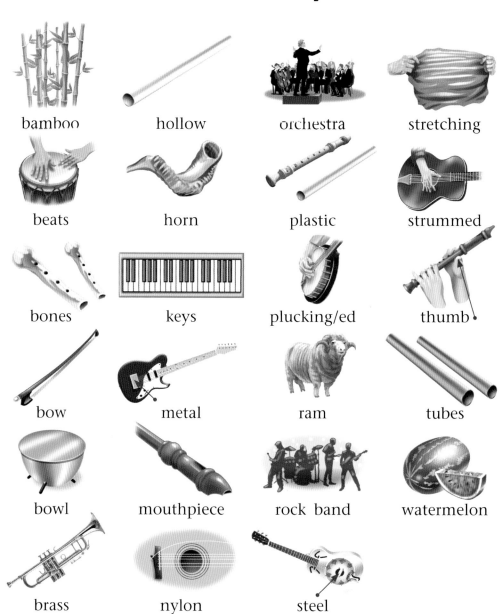

bamboo

hollow

orchestra

stretching

beats

horn

plastic

strummed

bones

keys

plucking/ed

thumb

bow

metal

ram

tubes

bowl

mouthpiece

rock band

watermelon

brass

nylon

steel